CONTENTS

ABOUT THE RECORDINGS

This icon (mp3) above a music example indicates that a FREE recording is available. All the recordings for this book can downloaded from Alfred-Music.com by typing the following link into a web browser:

http://alfred-music.com/MI/00-33580.zip

Save the file to your hard drive, then double-click and follow your computer's prompts to extract the mp3s and a PDF with more information about the recordings.

ACKNOWLEDGEMENTS

THANKS FROM JIMMY HASLIP

To my wife, Nancy, and family, Gabriela, Noah, Jason, and Beau, for all the love and support!

To ALFRED MUSIC: Aaron Stang, Glyn Dryhurst, Link Harnsberger, Mark Burgess, Doug Soulsby, Edgar Acosta, Lisa Mane, and Kate Westin (fabulous job on the editing Kate, you are the best!)

Keith Roscoe and Gard Lewis, ROSCOE GUITARS

Michael Tobias, MTD

Dave Avenius, AGUILAR

Darryl Anders, DUNLOP STRINGS

Ken Dapron, YAMAHA INT'L

Chris Campbell, ROCKBOX ELECTRONICS

BARTOLINI PICKUPS

Jack Thrift, MOODY GUITAR STRAPS

Hirotaka Kiuichi, INNERWOOD BASSES

Peter L. Janis, RADIAL ENGINEERING LTD.

Randy Fullmer, WYN BASSES

Pat Wilkins GUITARS

Rich Renkin, LINE 6, INC.

Greg Back & Allen Wald, THE BUZZY FEITEN TUNING SYSTEM

Ken Daniels & Paul Flynn, TRUE TONE MUSIC

Brian Vance, Frank Aresti, and Jim DiAddario, PLANET WAVES CABLES

INTRODUCTION

Improvising requires focused observation on some very fine points of study as well as dedication and commitment to your instrument. In my opinion, it involves improving your musicianship and constantly raising your bar of musical knowledge as well as finding a spiritual path that leads you to a connection between your passion and your heart. This will help you to inject your personality into your playing, creating a voice of some sort, and allow your spirituality to enter the music, which then gives the music a deeper expression! Extremely vital to this equation is your technical knowledge of music, which is much like learning a new language. The study of this language will allow you to communicate your emotions freely, and the more articulate you are, the clearer your audience will hear you. This is our goal to strive for in playing music. And you will realize that it is a gift!

Preparation and **study** are very important to reaching goals. Learning chord changes and song forms is a great way to prepare for playing music openly and for expanding your options. Doing so also opens the door to being comfortable with harmony and melody as it supports, strengthens, and builds confidence in your ability to improvise. The study of harmony is vast—actually, it's an infinite study. Studying everything that comes your way is essential to the growth of your musical vocabulary and also widens your scope of understanding music in general.

Study all you possibly can at your own pace. It is very important to **pay attention to your own learning pace.** Please don't be impatient. **Studying slow and methodically is actually preferred.** This will increase your ability to expand your musical boundaries. In the long run, with study and preparation, you will become more proficient and qualified to handle any musical situation. As a student in music, this direction will improve your self-motivation and continually build confidence within, creating a hunger to continue to progress and grow. This is something I feel is extremely important for perpetuating any type of career in music—from composers and arrangers to technicians, performers, and producers.

The **study and practice of composition** is also important and helpful in many ways. There are various approaches to composition. In the study of harmony, this can be another all-important tool for improving as a musician, adding another dimension and bringing an insightful element to your musicianship. Composing can open the door to writing in a stream-of-consciousness state and will be a very important factor in finding ideas that are unique.

For example…

Personally, I feel comfortable experimenting with rhythm first, and then finding harmonic structure that instinctually feels and sounds good as embellishment. Running a tape machine or something that can record your spur-of-the-moment ideas is a wonderful way to find some unique seeds that may ultimately become a completed composition.

I believe in taking music beyond the written pages of notes and accidentals so that I can communicate it on a deeper and more spiritual level. Practicing, studying, and being close to your instrument and sound help prepare you to achieve these goals. It's your spirituality that gives your music life!

Remember that the music is always the most important element here, and that **the song is a vehicle for expression.**

Very important: Always remember to stay relaxed!

When you're playing music, being relaxed is so important. The more relaxed you are, the better you will play. I employ breathing techniques and even use meditation to achieve a relaxed state of mind before a performance or session. Obviously, knowing the music ahead of time really helps as well. I try to make that happen as much as possible.

Study and preparation are, again, equally as important as staying relaxed. Breathing will keep you in the moment, but there's a balancing act to be aware of that involves where you are playing, the music at hand, and awareness of the musicians you are playing with. Breathing, being in the moment, staying in tune with the other musicians, listening to what's going on, locking into the entire situation with focus and concentration, being aware of my surroundings yet at the same time being in touch with my inner self, staying open to the spiritual experience of playing music, and channeling the music on an emotional level— that's what I strive for every time I play music. Those are my aspirations and what I hope to achieve every time. It's a wonderful life, and music is a gift.

A yoga instructor once told me that music is the highest form of yoga. This book is here to help us all focus on important study and preparation.

I wish you all my best and hope this material opens some doors toward success on any and all levels.

Jimmy Haslip

FUNDAMENTALS

The 12-Bar Blues

The 12-bar blues progression is one of the most fundamental and well-known structures in jazz and blues. Blues musicians tend to use phrases and patterns rather than scale runs, though jazz variations of blues can be based on a 12-bar blues structure and may include jazz and blues patterns alongside one another.

BASIC BLUES

Although some or all of the tonic and subdominant chords in the typical 12-bar blues progression may have a minor 7th added, this is a "blue" note, and it does not give the chords their usual dominant harmonic function. The exception is in bar 4 where the C7 chord acts a secondary dominant leading to the IV7 chord in bar 5.

The following example only introduces the 7th to the tonic at bar 4 to emphasize this chord change. It is not a modulation to IV as it would be in classical harmony.

Basic 12-Bar Blues Sequence   (mp3)01

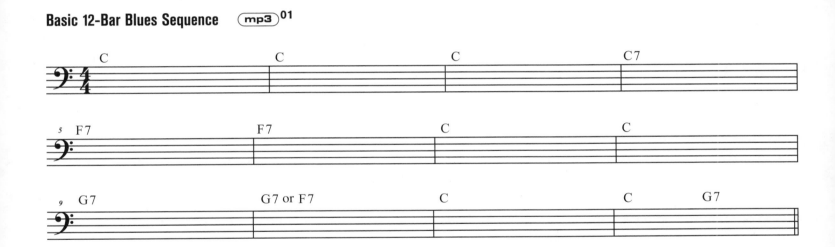

JAZZ/BLUES

A simple jazz/blues sequence usually changes the chord at bar 2 to IV and goes back to
chord I at bar 3. It also uses a IIm7 at bar 9 as a secondary dominant to the V7. This type
of sequence is typical of swing, jump, and R&B styles from the 1930s through the 1950s.

Early 12-Bar Jazz/Blues Sequence (mp3) 02

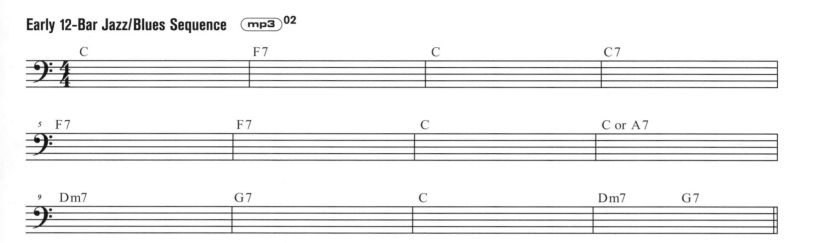

BEBOP

More complex sequences were used in bebop, as in the example below.

Typical Bebop Blues Changes (mp3) 03

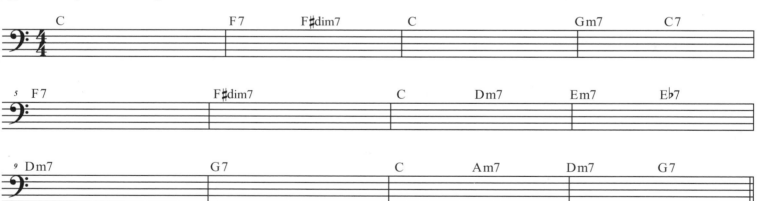

Rhythm Changes

The all-important progression known as *Rhythm Changes* has been a staple of jazz improvisation ever since Ira Gershwin wrote the song that became the template: "I've Got Rhythm." Originally composed as a slow song in 1928 for the musical *Treasure Girl*, it was later sped up and placed in the Broadway production *Girl Crazy*. The original song uses the pentatonic scale for its melody, but it's the 32-bar chord progression that became the standard form for a variety of songs written from the bebop era to the present day.

Rhythm Changes was also used extensively by bebop legend Charlie Parker to write countless original songs and melodies that have become standards in many a fake book. I recommend studying this formula very diligently. By knowing it inside and out, you will add a large number of tunes to your personal repertoire and increase your melodic vocabulary for soloing—very important! In fact, there is a book, *The Charlie Parker Omnibook*, written for bass clef instruments, that I suggest you have for this purpose—it's a very important study tool that will seriously improve your phrasing and melodic ideas for soloing.

It's extremely important to understand Rhythm Changes before digging in to playing. Here is a list of songs that use Rhythm Changes. It's a good idea to listen to at least a few of these to get the sound in your ears.

Allen's Alley (a.k.a. **Wee**) by Denzil Best

Almost by David Baker

Anthropology (a.k.a. **Thrivin' on a Riff**)
    by Charlie Parker/Dizzy Gillespie

Apple Honey by Woody Herman

Bop-Kick by Nat King Cole

Boppin' a Riff by Sonny Stitt

Brown Gold by Art Pepper

Bud's Bubble by Bud Powell

Call the Police by Nat King Cole

Calling Dr. Jazz by Eddie "Lockjaw" Davis

Celebrity by Charlie Parker

Chant of the Groove by Coleman Hawkins

Chasin' the Bird by Charlie Parker

Cheers by Charlie Parker

Constellation by Charlie Parker

Coolie-Rini by Howard McGhee

Coppin' the Bop by J.J. Johnson

Cotton Tail by Duke Ellington

Delirium by Tadd Dameron

Dexterity by Charlie Parker

Dexter's Deck by Dexter Gordon

Dorothy by Howard McGhee

The Duel by Dexter Gordon

Duke by Ulf Wakenius

Eb Pob by Fats Navarro/Leo Parker

Fat Girl by Fats Navarro

Fifty Second Street Theme
    by Thelonious Monk

Flat Out by John Scofield

The Flintstones Theme by Hoyt Curtin

Fox Hunt by J.J. Johnson

Goin' to Minton's by Fats Navarro

Good Queen Bess by Duke Ellington

The Goof and I by Al Cohn

Harlem Swing by Nat King Cole

Hawes Paws by Hampton Hawes

Hollerin' and Screamin'
    by Eddie "Lockjaw" Davis

I'm an Errand Boy for Rhythm
    by Nat King Cole

In Walked Horace by J.J. Johnson

Jay Jay Jaybird by J.J. Johnson

The Jeep is Jumpin' by Duke Ellington

Jug Handle by Gene Ammons

Juggernaut by Gene Ammons

Juggin' Around by Frank Foster

Jumpin' at the Woodside by Count Basie

Lemon Drop by George Wallington

Lester Leaps In by Lester Young

Lilla Mae by Nat King Cole

The Man on the Little White Keys
    by Nat King Cole

Miss Thing by Count Basie

Moody Speaks (original version)
    by James Moody / Dave Burns

Moody's Got Rhythm by James Moody

Moose the Mooch by Charlie Parker

Mop, Mop by Gaillard/Stewart/Tatum

Newk's Fadeaway by Sonny Rollins

No Moe by Sonny Rollins

Oleo by Sonny Rollins

One Bass Hit by Dizzy Gillespie

An Oscar for Treadwell by Dizzy Gillespie

Passport by Charlie Parker

Red Cross by Charlie Parker

Rhythm-a-Ning by Thelonious Monk

Rhythm in a Riff by Billy Eckstine

Rhythm Sam by Nat King Cole

Salt Peanuts by Dizzy Gillespie

Seven Come Eleven by Charlie Christian

Shag by Sidney Bechet

Shaw Nuff by Dizzy Gillespie

Shoe Shine Boy by Lester Young

Sonny Side Up by Sonny Stitt

Squatty Roo by Johnny Hodges

Stay On It by Tadd Dameron

Steeplechase by Charlie Parker

Straighten Up and Fly Right
    by Nat King Cole

Strictly Confidential by Bud Powell

Suspone by Mike Stern

Swingin' with Diane by Art Pepper

Swing Spring by J.J. Johnson

Syntax by J.J. Johnson

The Theme by Miles Davis

Tiptoe by Thad Jones

Turnpike by J.J. Johnson

Unchanged Rhythm by Joe Diorio

Wail by Bud Powell

Webb City by Bud Powell

Wee (a.k.a. **Allen's Alley**) by Dizzy Gillespie

Who's Who? by Art Farmer

Wire Brush Stomp by Gene Krupa

XYZ by Budd Johnson

THE RHYTHM CHANGES PROGRESSION

Rhythm Changes is a 32-bar chord progression in A–A–B–A form, as shown here in the key of B♭.

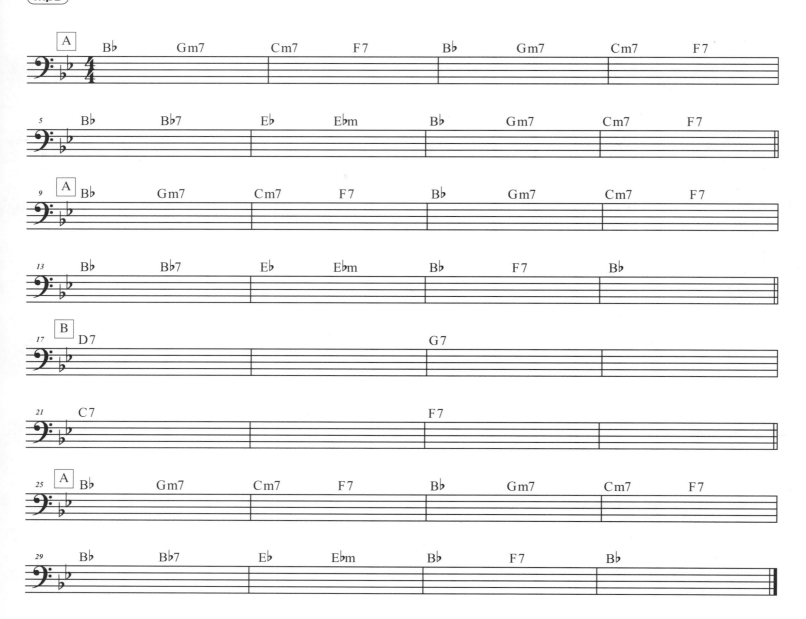

THE A SECTION

The basic structure of the A section is a diatonic I–VI–II–V progression. The following suggestions work well for improvising over these chords.

- B♭ major scale
- F bebop scale: F G A B♭ C D E♭ E F
- G minor pentatonic scale
- Arpeggios and melodic patterns from the above scales

The following interesting alternative to the A section gives you some additional choices for improvising. Notice that the Gm7 from bars 3 and 7 has been substituted with G7, and in bar 1, the Gm7 is substituted by a Bdim7 (same as a G7♭9) instead of G7 to get the chromatic line to Cm7. In bar 2, the C♯dim7 is, in fact, also called A7♭9, and continues the chromatic line initiated in bar 1 through to the Dm7 in bar 3.

mp3 05

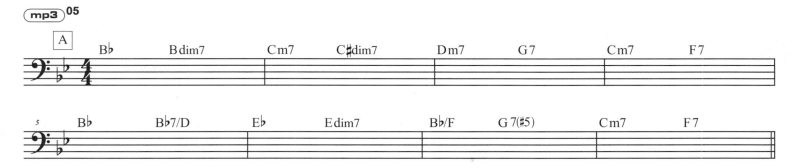

The following is another commonly used variation of the A section. Notice here that the diminished chords in the altered version above are now altered forms of the original dominants. In bar 5, the vertical movement is all in fourths in the bass with the chords Fm7, B♭7(♭9), E♭maj7, and A♭7(♯11). Then, in bar 6, the A♭7♯11 is the tritone substitution for D7, which is the V of G7 in bar 7.

mp3 06

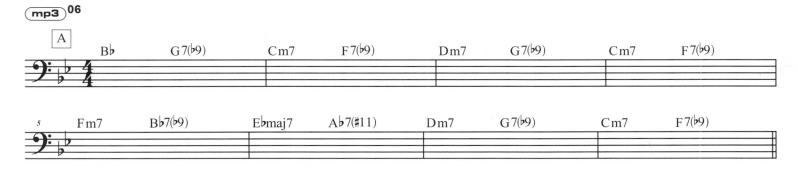

THE B SECTION

The B section of Rhythm Changes is the bridge, and it uses secondary dominants. To reach the F7 at the end of this section, which is the primary dominant in the tonality of B♭ major, it is preceded by its dominant, C7. This C7 is preceded by its dominant, G7, which is set up by its dominant, D7, at the start of the bridge.

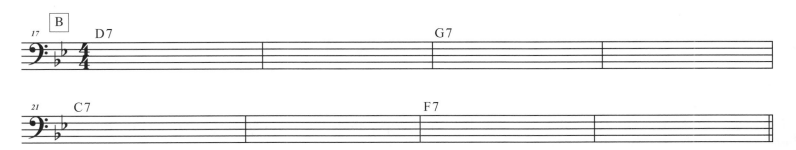

For improvising, try the following scales over the chords of the bridge:
- **D7: D Mixolydian**
- **G7: G Mixolydian / G altered**
- **C7: C Mixolydian**
- **F7: F Mixolydian / F altered**

THE BACK CYCLE
Putting the II chord in the measure before the V chord gives you what's called a *back cycle*. This creates an interesting variation of the B section, shown below.

TRITONE SUBSTITUTION
We can also use the tritone substition for all the dominants to get a chromatic bridge.

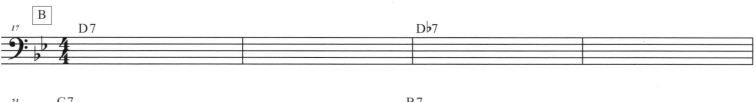

ADDING THE II CHORD
Another interesting harmonic option to expand your improvisational palette is to add the II chord into the sequence, as shown here.

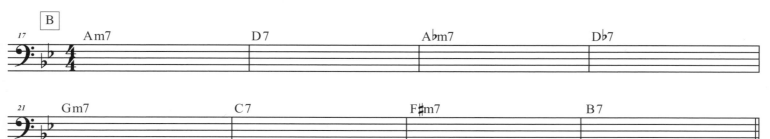

The II–V–I

HARMONIC SUBSTITUTION AND THE II–V–I: "RUN FOR YOUR LIFE"

Now let's look at a song form that has several II–V–I progressions. This particular song, "Run for Your Life," was written by Bob Mintzer, the saxophonist with the Yellowjackets, using Rhythm Changes as a template. Below is the chart showing the song in its basic, traditional form.

Run for Your Life

mp3 10

By BOB MINTZER

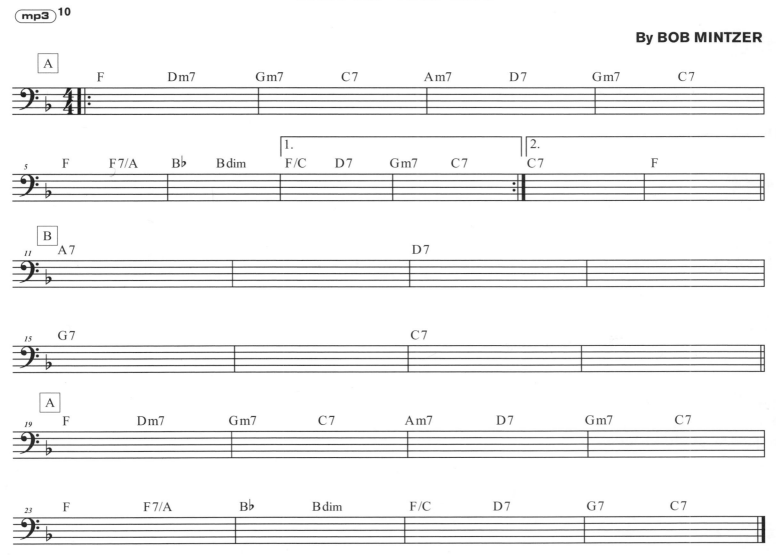

Jimmy Haslip: Modern Improvisation for Bass

ERRATA

The chord progression for example 12 (Tritone Substitution) on page 15 is incorrect. The chords should be Em7, Eb7, Am7, D7, Dm7, Db7, Gm7 and C7. There is one chord per measure. We apologize for any inconvenience this may have caused, and the error will be corrected on future printings.

Note that letter B is loaded with II–V–I movements. One rule you can apply to this section is substituting the II chords of the progression (in this case, starting with an Em7) and following them with the V chords (in this case, starting with an A7). Then, the B section will look like this:

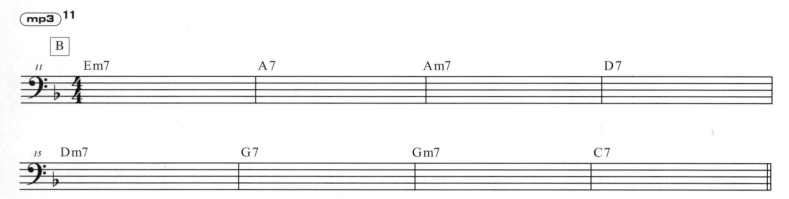

As you can see, this substitution method will supply a series of four II–V turnarounds that will eventually lead you back to the original key of the song, which is F major.

TRITONE SUBSTITUTION

Here's another harmonic alteration to consider. Try substituting the A7 chord with the E♭7. This is a *tritone substitution*, meaning the substitution of a chord with a dominant chord that has its root a tritone away from the original. The tritone substitution is one of the most common substitutions found in jazz, and it was the precursor to more complex substitution patterns like Coltrane changes. Tritone substitutions are often used in improvisation to create tension during a solo. Using another tritone substitution of the G7 with D♭7, now the B section would look something like this:

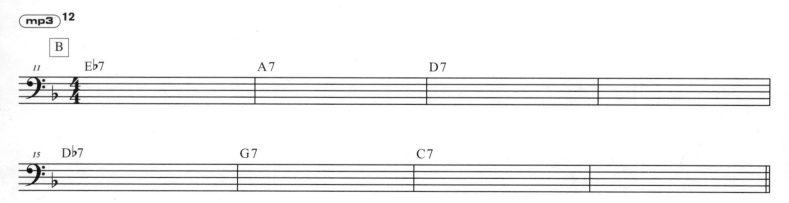

This works because the 3rd and 7th intervals of the original chord and its substitutions are interchangeable: E♭7 has G as its major 3rd and D♭ as its 7th, while A7 has G as its 7th and D♭ as its major 3rd; D♭7 has F as its major 3rd and B as its 7th, while G7 has F as its 7th and B as its major 3rd.

"RUN FOR YOUR LIFE": A STUDY OF RHYTHM CHANGES

Harmonic and Melodic Analysis

It is important for all musicians to understand the II–V–I progression, which is commonly used in so many songs. A hard practice regime of study will lead to eventually knowing the II–V–I progression inside out, and this will give you a new lease on life as a confident soloist.

The study of the II–V–I progression in conjunction with Rhythm Changes will also give you a good foundation for the study of song form in general and help you in learning all songs in the future. It will definitely improve your sense of harmony!

I have given you a lot of the basic rules and also some altered approaches to soloing over the basic II–V–I progression, which will help you get started with a formulaic approach to soloing or playing through these changes. The chart of chord changes for "Run for Your Life" on page 14 was provided so you could see what it looks like on paper, and now you can examine each chord to see how all the harmonic information given to you fits together. It will give you a clear picture of how all of these particular rules are applied.

Remember that the Rhythm Changes formula is A–A–B–A. This means that there are three A melody sections that are repetitions of the same harmony, and one B section, also known as the *bridge*, with a different harmonic structure. Each section is 8 bars long, and the entire song form equals 32 bars of music.

Now, this is only part of the available information you can learn from the studying of a song. I suggest that we look at and study *all* the available information in order to see the big picture and understand the song in its entirety. A single song can teach you so much, and we can take advantage of that knowledge simply by applying ourselves and spending some serious practice time dissecting the music and all of its components.

To that end, we need to study the song in its totality. I was taught to learn all of the parts of a song. If you know the melody, the chords, the bass line, and the basic rhythms played by the percussionist and/or the drummer, then, *and only then*, will you really know the complete song and be able to play it exceptionally well as a bassist. You will also be prepared harmonically and rhythmically to take a solo on that song. This study habit can be applied to any song in any genre, and believe me—it works. It's a way to improve your musicianship and eliminate any kind of guessing game when it comes to playing the music.

As mentioned, the previous chart of "Run for Your Life" was written out with the basic traditional Rhythm Changes form in mind, but when this song was written for the Yellowjackets' album of the same name, an extra section was included. This additional 32-bar section is also known as a *kicker*. It is a compositional tool that alters the form of Rhythm Changes by extending it to 64 bars. The harmony is basically the same throughout, adding more II–V–I progressions to the form so the soloist can improvise on this section as well. This technique provides a slingshot effect for the solo section, giving the soloist a running start, so to speak. It builds momentum so that the soloist can launch into the actual solo section, which is the traditional A–A–B–A song form.

The following chart shows the complete 64-bar form, including the kicker, of "Run for Your Life" as written for the album.

Run for Your Life
As Performed by the Yellowjackets

By BOB MINTZER

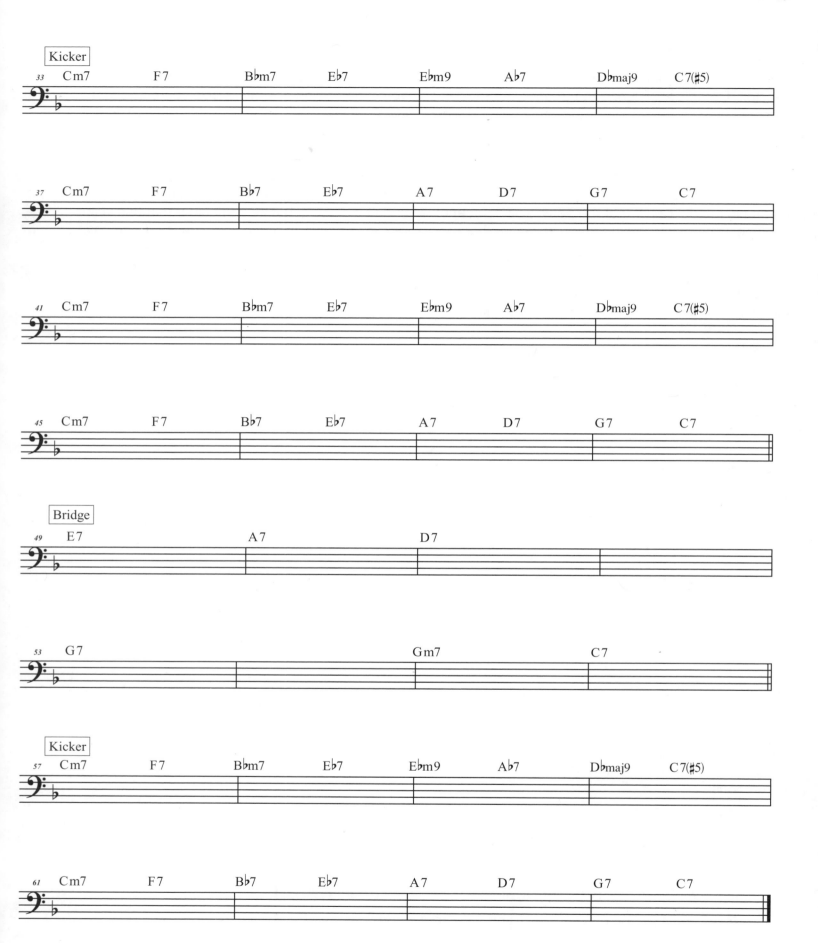

THE HARMONY

The preceding complete chord chart of "Run for Your Life" was written for the Yellowjackets' recording session. Compare this chart to the one on page 14, and you can see how the alternative chord changes work in place of the straight traditional chord changes, thus stretching the harmonic possibilities. You will also see how the kicker section alters the tradition, but adds new dimension to the composition without eliminating the original song form.

Let's first review the chordal harmony and go deep inside these substitutions before moving on to the melody. We're going to examine the information carefully and enjoy experimenting on this truly great harmonic puzzle. Know that the possibilities are endless and challenging, but also consider that this is an extremely interesting way to study advanced harmony. This can, and will, improve your sense of harmony.

Looking at the excerpt below, notice that there are some variations in the chord changes between the first eight bars at A1 and the second eight bars at A2. But you should know that the harmony is basically the same; it's just altered some to create a slightly different coloration in this harmonic accompaniment. Let's glance at the alterations to see how this works.

Compare A1 to A2 and you will see where the altered harmony is used. Since these sections are a mirror image of one another's form and basic harmony, you can simply compare them bar by bar to expose their differences.

Bar 2 vs. 10: You can see that we have an A♭dim in place of the C7. The notes in the C7 are C, E, G, B♭ and the notes in the A♭dim are A♭, B, D, F.

Bar 5 vs. 13: You can see that we have an F7 in place of a Cm7 and an A7 in place of an F7. The notes in the F7 are F, A, C, E♭, and the notes in the Cm7 are C, E♭, G, B♭. The notes in the A7 are A, C♯, E, G, and, again the notes in the F7 are F, A, C, E♭.

Bar 7 vs. 15: You can see a C7 and a D7 replaced by just the C7. Again, the notes in the C7 are C, E, G, B♭, and the notes in the D7 are D, F♯, A, C. The C7 is used for the entire bar 15.

Bar 8 vs. 16: You can see a G7 and C7 replaced an F7. The notes in the G7 are G, B, D, F, and the C7 is C, E, G, B♭. These chords are now replaced by the F7 which is the notes F, A, C, E♭.

THE MELODY

Now for the melody. Let's look at the extended harmony created when you combine the chord changes with the corresponding melody, which is included in the chart below.

Run for Your Life
As Performed by the Yellowjackets

By BOB MINTZER

22

SECTION A2

Bar 9: The melody starts on beat 1 with an F note, the root of the F7 chord it is played against. After two quarter rests, the second melody note is a B♭ on beat 4, which is a ♯5 against the D7 chord. (Note: this can be interpreted as an upper-degree chordal scale tone, which is called a *tension* or *extension tone*. In this case, it would be the ♭13th degree.)

Bars 10 and 11: After a two-beat rest, there is a G note on beat 3 and a D note on beat 4 against the A♭dim chord. Here we have the major 7th and the ♭5 (or ♯11) of the chord. Notice that the D is tied and hangs over to beat 1 of bar 11, where it becomes the 4th (or 11th), and on beat 2 you have a B♮ as the major 2nd (or 9th) against an A7 chord. On beat 3, we have a C note, the dominant 7th of the D7 chord, and a quarter note rest to finish the bar.

Bar 12: On beat 1, we have an eighth rest, then A♭, B♮, and E notes against a G7 chord, which are, respectively, the ♭2 (or ♭9), the major 3rd, and the 6th (or 13th). Then we have the four eighth notes high G, E, F, and C, all against a C7 chord: they are the perfect 5th, major 3rd, the 4th (or 11th), and the root (or octave).

Bars 13 and 14: The C note from bar 12 is tied and hangs over to bar 13, beat 1, and on beat 2 is an A note, both against the F7 chord; they are the 5th and the 3rd intervals of the chord. After another quarter rest, an F note on beat 4 is the ♯5 (or ♭13) against the A7 chord. Bar 14 starts with a two-beat rest, then over a B♭7 chord we have a B♭ note and an F note, which are the root and 5th. Then an A♭ note (enharmonically a G♯) is the 6th (or 13th) interval over a Bdim chord.

Bar 15: The A♭ is tied and hangs over into bar 15, and then we also have three more eighth notes: an A♮, another A♭, and another A♮ against the C7 chord. The A♭ is the ♯5, and the A♮ is the 6th (or 13th).

Bar 16: A four-beat rest creates a space with no melody to set up the bridge section.

THE BRIDGE

Now for the bridge section. This 8-bar B section is a release from the three A sections (A1, A2, and approaching A3). This section provides a breath of air and gives the song a new harmonic point of view.

Bar 17: The first bar of the bridge has an E note on beat 1, followed by a quarter rest, then a B♮ and a D note against an Em7 chord. So you have the root, the 5th, and the minor 7th spelling out the basic chord.

Bar 18: After an eighth rest, a high F♯ note, and an A, there are the four eighth notes F♮, D♭, C, and B♭, all against an A7 chord: the F♯ is the 6th (or the 13th), the A is the root, the F♮ is the ♯5, the D♭ (enharmonically a C♯) is the major 3rd, the C is the minor 3rd (or the ♯9), and the B♭ is the minor 2nd (or ♭9).

Bar 19: The notes A, E, and D are followed by a two-beat rest against a D7 chord. They are the 5th, the major 2nd (or 9th), and the root.

Bar 20: The notes E♭, B♭, and A♭ against the D7 chord are the minor 2nd (or ♭9), the minor 6th or 13th (or ♯5), and the ♭5 (or ♯11). This particular note selection constitutes a very melodic, yet altered, sound.

Bar 21: Here we have an F, a quarter rest, a D♭, and an E against a G7 chord: the F is the dominant 7th, the D♭ is the ♭5 (or ♯11), and the E is the 6th (or 13th).

Bar 22: After an eighth rest, there is a high A, C♯, B♮, another A, an E, and another C♯ against the G7: the A's are 9th intervals, the C♯'s are ♯11's, the B is the major 3rd (or 10th), and the E is the 6th (or 13th).

Bar 23: The note G is followed by an A, B♭, quarter rest, and D♭ against a Gm7 chord. This means we have the root (or octave), the 9th, the minor 3rd (or the 10th), and the ♭5 (or ♯11).

Bar 24: Here there's an E♭ and an F♭ (enharmonically E♮), followed by a quarter rest and a half rest against a C7 chord. So now we have the ♯9 in the E♭ and major 3rd, which can also be looked at as the 10th interval.

Just to point out an interesting observation (if you haven't already noticed), bars 9, 10, and 11 are rhythmically identical to bars 1, 2, and 3. You'll notice that bars 21, 22, 23, and 24 are almost identical in rhythm to bars 17, 18, 19, and 20. The only difference is the rhythm of the three notes in bar 20 that are displaced and appear in a similar rhythmic pattern starting on beat 4 of bar 23 and ending on beat 1 of bar 24. In other words, the last three notes of the melodic structure have simply been moved over by one quarter note, creating an interesting pattern to complete the bridge section.

SECTION A3

Section A3 is exactly the same as section A1, just using some slight alterations in the chord changes. The melody is exactly the same, except for the last bar (bar 32), where there's no melody. The space created by the rest sets up the next section, the kicker, which then launches the solo sections.

THE KICKER

Melodically, the kicker is played as a series of accents. There is a note played with each chord change, all in the upper intervallic structure of the chords.

Bar 33: There are two half notes: the F against the Cm7 chord is the 11th, and the D against the F7 chord is the 13th.

Bar 34: Again there are two half notes: an E♭ is the 11th against the B♭m7 chord, and the C is the 13th of the E♭7 chord.

Bar 35: A B♭ is the 5th against an E♭m9 chord, and F is the 13th against an A♭7 chord.

Bar 36: The A♭ against the D♭maj9 chord is the 5th, and the E♭ against the C7♯5 chord is the ♯9.

This covers the entire melody of this piece and should give you a very broad and complete view of the harmony used in composing this song. Dissecting a song in this way allows you to examine every little nuance in depth and will ultimately give you the proverbial key to solving this melodic and rhythmic puzzle. Learning a song in this fashion also allows you to experiment and improvise without question. You have unlocked the door—now enter and observe the song from within. Work on this melody in its entirety and get comfortable playing it. You are now the lead instrument, so picture playing this in unison with the saxophone.

DEVELOPING THE WALKING BASS LINE

Now that we've dissected and studied the chord changes and melody of "Run for Your Life" in depth, their relationship is very clear, and you should have a good understanding of what is going on with the Rhythm Changes form. Again, I'll stress the importance of this song form and why it's so important to know it inside out. For starters, you'll become comfortable with a complex form that includes these natural II–V turnarounds and gain insight into leading tones for any songs you may be performing. Secondly, you will be able to play any of the hundreds of songs that are written with this chord progression, because the only differences among them is in the melodies. Thirdly, elements of the II–V–I progression are used in virtually every possible kind of music as a writing tool. So we've covered a lot of ground when it comes to applying this harmonic knowledge to whatever music you may perform.

It's also important to develop and study walking patterns using this harmonic structure to create a better understanding of the harmony itself. The objective here is also to increase your ability to walk freely through these changes. The melodic possibilities in both the harmonic and rhythmic structure are endless, and we should definitely explore these possibilities as much as we can. **Increase your options at all times by studying and practicing walking bass lines on this chord progression!**

I like to practice walking through these changes with just a drum machine or metronome. If you can do this until you are totally comfortable and making all the harmony clear, your playing will improve. Also, it is important to have the melody memorized so you can hear it clearly in your head. This will allow you to keep your place in the tune structure without relying on anything or anyone else. It's important to be as independent as possible when playing music so that you can become a rock-solid musician, making the group that much stronger—and you'll find it will show growth with your improvisational skills. It will also enhance any music you are performing and give the other musicians the freedom to explore as well without concern. This makes you an important part of the group's chemistry!

Now, let's take a look at the walking bass line, which is the type of groove used in performing "Run for Your Life." This style of jazz music has the bassist playing through the chord changes using swinging eighth note patterns. The walking bass pattern propels the music and provides the accompaniment for the drummer's swinging style of groove. It also complements the chordal and melodic instruments with a continuous melodic counterpoint of harmonic phrases.

Here are some basic rules to follow when developing a walking bass line:

1. Always establish the harmony clearly in the bass, especially during a solo without chordal accompaniment.

2. Always make sure that the roots, or at least the 3rds or 5ths, are played on the downbeats at the beginning of the chordal phrases. Look at bars 1, 3, 5, and 7 to apply this rule.

3. It's important to work on your phrasing and keep the time strong, even without a drummer playing, so practice walking through these changes. Slow is good at first, or you can establish a comfortable tempo for yourself. Practicing with a metronome or a drum machine is a good way to start things off.

The goal is to be able to play through these chord changes effortlessly in a confident manner without any assistance. This will guarantee that, with or without accompaniment, you'll be able to walk musically and support the song completely on your own. Developing your confidence and familiarity with this chord progression will generate good time and meaningful phrasing—all in the name of a clear, creative harmonic statement.

The Modes

To get our bearings straight, let's re-examine the chord progression of the A1 section of "Run for Your Life" (page 18). Notice that I have marked each chord with a Roman numeral that signifies its relationship to the tonic chord, which, in this case, is the F7 chord.

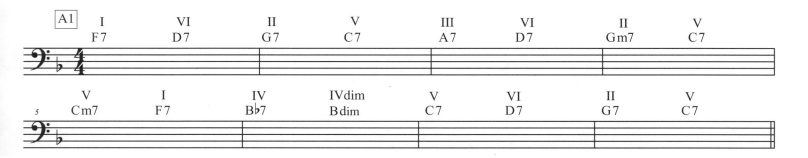

Although some of the chords in the progression are not diatonic, including the root chord F7, many of them are, so one way you can approach these A section 8-bar chord progressions is with the *modal scale system*. The modes are very useful in constructing walking bass patterns by simply using the major/minor diatonic system and its relative scales. The seven modes all share the same exact notes, because they are basically the same scale in seven different positions or inversions. This combination of scales allows you to create a walking bass line that is diatonically correct with the chords that are diatonic in the A sections of "Run for Your Life." Remember that there are three A sections in this song, the song form being A–A–B–A, and therefore the same scale systems will work on all three!

THE MODES IN THE KEY OF F (mp3)¹⁵

Here are chord changes to use over these modes:

F Ionian: Fmaj7	C Mixolydian: Cmaj7
G Dorian: Gm	D Aeolian: Dm7
A Phrygian: Adim	E Locrian: Em7
Bb Lydian: Bbmaj(b5)	

Altered Harmony Using the Chromatic Scale

THE CHROMATIC SCALE

Another application for designing a walking bass line is found in altering the harmony and looking at the substitution chords. Here are a few ways that the harmony is altered using the chromatic scale, and how we can build a walking bass line with this interesting sound.

Chromatic Scale on F

Check out the next example. You have the option of altering the first two bars of the phrase by using the chromatic scale: from F, the tonic note; to F♯, which is the major 3rd of the D7 chord; then to G, which is the root of the II chord (G7); to a G♯, which is the major 3rd of an E7 chord. E7 substitutes for the C7 and leads to the A7 chord perfectly, thus creating additional harmony with a V-to-I chord relationship, all by using the chromatic scale. Bars 6 and 7 have a built-in chromatic movement that's all part of this same scale.

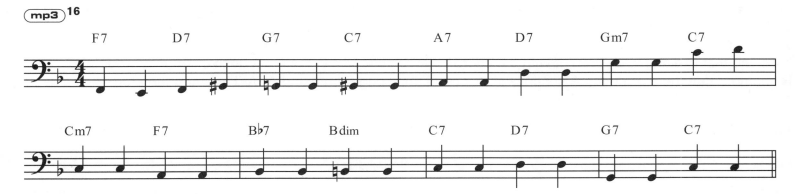

CHROMATIC NON-HARMONIC TONES

Notes that are moved in a chromatic fashion create altered harmonic values to chords and scales. This chromatic altering can also be utilized in improvisation to create tension and dissonance in an improvised solo. We can look at this chromatic movement as interesting passing tones—or a bridging—between diatonic structure and movement. These notes are called *non-harmonic tones* and create infinite options to any improvisation.

One rule of thumb is to provide essential intervallic notes on a strong beat, meaning the *downbeats*, of the chords in cadence. This helps to strongly suggest the existing harmony in resolution, giving the improvisation balance and confirming the harmonic structure. But even this rule has its breaking point because of the rhythmic and melodic open options in altering the melodic phrases. This, of course, can give the improvisation more personality and a unique twist. Please keep these thoughts in mind. With exploration, you can then experiment to find your voice—your personal expression.

Check out the exercise below. Study Dm7, G7, and Cmaj7. Notice the first two notes of each phrase and that this progression has a built-in harmonic structure that can be chromatically altered.

Pentatonic Scales (5-Note Scales)

Another harmonic tool related to the major/minor diatonic system is the *pentatonic scale system* ("penta" being ancient Greek for the number five, and "tonic" meaning the pitch that is the tonal center). This is a basic system of five scales consisting of five notes each. Combining this scale system with the blues scale system and the modal system provides plenty of options to help you build some impressive walking bass patterns and allows you to improvise without second-guessing your note selections.

PENTATONIC SCALES IN F MAJOR / D MINOR (mp3)[18]

Root Position (1st Inversion Dm)

1st Inversion (2nd Inversion Dm)

2nd Inversion (3rd Inversion Dm)

3rd Inversion (4th Inversion Dm)

4th Inversion (Root Position Dm)

Pentatonic scales are used in almost all genres of music, especially cultural folk music, around the world. Because they are a great vehicle for creating interesting and uniquely dynamic melodic and rhythmic patterns, these scales are also cornerstones in most improvisational music like rock, blues, jazz, and progressive rock. Pentatonic scales are designed to be extremely versatile and harmonically flexible, with compatibility and openness to any melodic structure. They can also create tension and even dissonant expression when used as altered scales, hinged on placement and note selection. This all depends on harmonic information such as dominant chords within the composition.

(mp3) 19

Here's a good series of pentatonic scales to get comfortable with because it will open the door to finding some unique patterns of your own. Be sure to alter these examples both melodically and rhythmically. The Kumoi and Sen scales are Japanese pentatonic scales, presented here to expand your harmonic palette.

Dm7(♭5)

F Kumoi

F Minor Pentatonic

A♭ Major Pentatonic

G in Sen

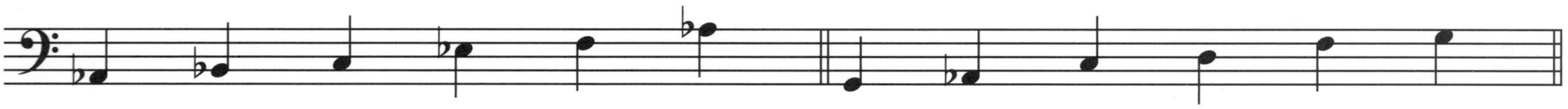

B♭ Major Pentatonic

E♭ Major Pentatonic

G13

G Major Pentatonic

E Minor Pentatonic

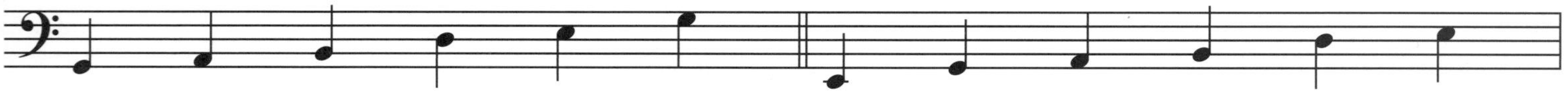

G7

D Minor Pentatonic

D Kumoi

G7(♯9)

G Minor Pentatonic

B♭ Major Pentatonic

G7sus4(♭9)

F Kumoi

G in Sen

G7alt

Ab Kumoi

Db Major Pentatonic

Bb Minor Pentatonic

Eb Major Pentatonic

G13(b9)

G Major Pentatonic (b2)

Bb Major Pentatonic (b2)

Db Major Pentatonic (b2)

E Major Pentatonic (b2)

G7sus4

D Minor Pentatonic

F Major Pentatonic

A Minor Pentatonic

Here is an exercise using major pentatonic scales. Play the bass line against the chords on keyboard or with the MP3 to explore improvisation.

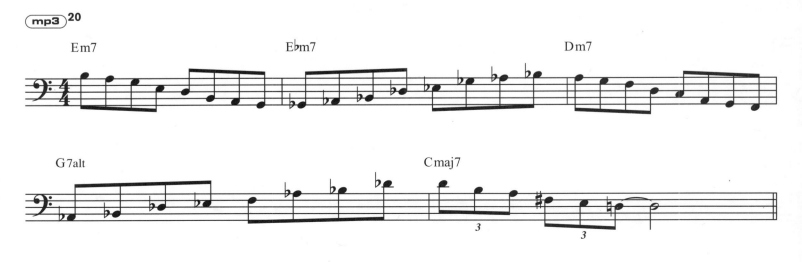

mp3 20

Em7   Ebm7   Dm7

G7alt   Cmaj7

Here are some rapid passages of pentatonic scales with triplet patterns.

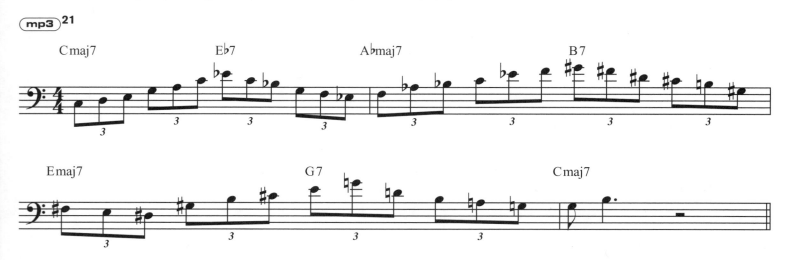

You should also try pulling these corresponding chord changes apart. There is interesting harmonic information here, and it's always a good idea to study the chord structure of any progression to discover the important harmonic information you can rely upon to add dimension to the study of each exercise. This will also inspire you to explore your own ways of altering the exercises.

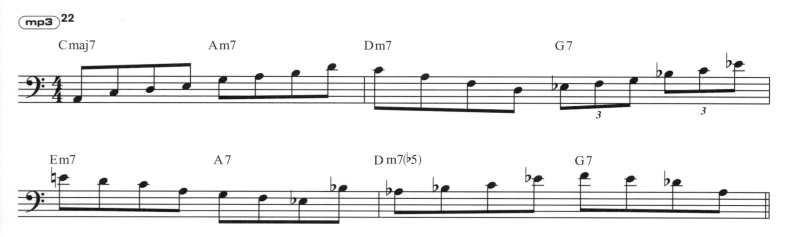

Here is yet another interesting exercise using pentatonics in an altered state. Focus on the A13♭9 chord with the E♭ minor pentatonic scale, and the G7 altered chord with the D♭ major pentatonic scale. The G7alt can have the added altered tones ♭9, ♯9, ♭5, or ♯5. (Altered chords are based on chromatically altering these intervals.)

A13♭9 = A C♯ E G B♭ F♯   **G7alt** = G B D F
             1   3   5 ♭7 ♭9 13   1 3 5 ♭7

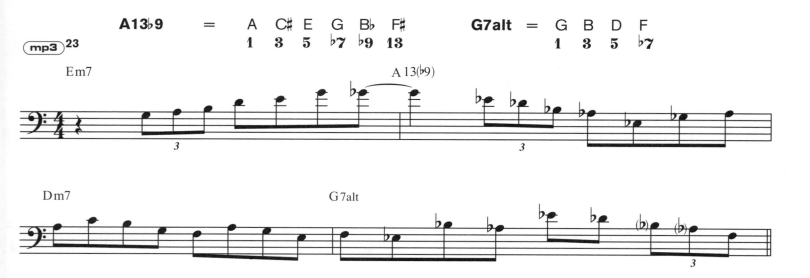

Rhythmic Choices

Now that we've examined some of the harmonic and melodic possibilities of "Run for Your Life," let's look at some of the rhythmic possibilities.

TRIPLETS

Since we're dealing with a basic, straight-four rhythm here, the time signature is 4/4. You can choose to stay in four in conjunction with the four quarter notes in the bar, or you can choose to play some triplet note figures by superimposing two sets of quarter note triplets over the four beats in the bar. This will give you some interesting rhythmic choices to begin with, as seen below.

PLAYING IN HALF TIME

Another way to add rhythmic dynamic to your walking bass line is to play in half time, like the next example demonstrates. This will allow you to create an interesting contrast within a very up-tempo song such as "Run for Your Life." It also creates a simple polyrhythmic feel and definitely builds tension into the groove. You can also do the opposite by playing a double-time walking bass line while performing a song in a slower tempo.

PEDAL TONES

Another way to stir things up and make your accompaniment more interesting is to play pedal tones under the chord changes, as in the next example. This will really bring the groove to a boiling point and allow the music to open up and expand, especially for the soloist.

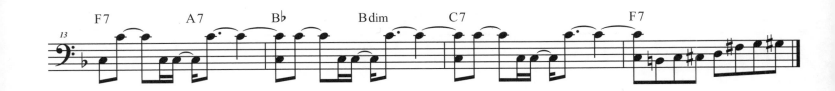

BREAKING UP THE RHYTHM

The next example demonstrates a rhythmic twist that can add excitement to a walking bass line by simply breaking up the rhythm randomly as you play it. Skipping beats and ghosting notes are useful techniques, and slurring or sliding notes will achieve interesting results as well. This will again create rhythmic dynamics with the other musicians and give the music more accented punctuation throughout, creating a topography of peaks and valleys instead of a flat and straight landscape with no points of interest. You want to be able to improvise and make it as interesting as possible. This will give the music more meaning and passion.

Keep in mind that the four preceding examples I've given are just a few possible ideas exhibited as "ways to walk" through these changes. There are many more possibilities, and aside from exploring them, it's also my advice to listen to as many recordings of Rhythm Changes as you can to hear the most ideas performed by as many different bass players as possible. This, in combination with the examples I've given you, will create a good foundation to start your exploration, and hopefully it will inspire and motivate you in your search for insight into building your walking bass vocabulary. That's all it takes. Study hard and practice, and you will surely be rewarded for your efforts!

All of this information is helpful in the infinite learning process of this improvisational language, and the goal here is to broaden your ability to use this language in the same way you might carry on a conversation with a friend—the key to a meaningful improvisational outcome.

Walking Through the Bridge

Now let's explore some ideas for building a walking bass line throughout the B section, the bridge of our Rhythm Changes piece. Here are the changes (see page 19).

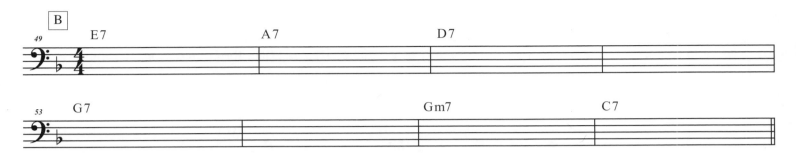

There are many ways to approach this section, and the following three examples illustrate some of my ideas. These are just a few suggestions of places to start in order to get comfortable with walking through these bridge chord changes.

1. Use chromatic patterns to walk over the bridge section.

2. Use the basic chord spelling, and play patterns using the triads of each corresponding chord.

3. Use patterns formed with the modes in mind. The example below uses the respective Mixolydian modes.

I know that by using these ideas as a jumping-off point, you will be able to open the door creatively and start to compile other possible ways of walking over these bridge changes. **Remember:** This chord progression is used quite frequently in many songs in all different styles of music. By exploring the possibilities of walking bass lines here, you are also exploring the harmonic possibilities of all other songs, no matter what genre, using these chord movements.

ALTERED VARIATIONS OF RHYTHM CHANGES

Music is an amazing study. At times, I've spent years studying just one or two songs, scale groups, and melodic concepts. I have benefited from such intense studying, and it has become a way for me to play music from deep down inside the depths of my soul. Through spending intimate time with your instrument and searching for answers about how to approach and understand the music you play and enjoy, you will constantly increase your level of musicianship and achieve success in your growth as a musician.

Up to now, we've been concentrating on a single song. I'd like to continue our study of Rhythm Changes by exploring different songs and melodies in order to discover the many harmonic possibilities for building walking bass lines, and thus open the door to freely soloing over these changes. You'll be introduced to more harmonic information in the form of altered versions of Rhythm Changes, with changes in the actual structure and altered harmonic possibilities. While we were in the key of F during this entire study of the slightly altered Rhythm Changes piece "Run for Your Life," now we'll look at more severely altered variations as well as other pieces in different keys.

Rhythm Changes are most commonly played in the keys of F, B♭, C, and E♭. As we look at all these keys, I recommend that you transcribe any or all the melodic information in the previous lessons to these other keys as an exercise.

Bebop Scales

Let's start with four new scales to add to your personal melodic library that I think will be helpful through the chordal sequences of Rhythm Changes. These scales supply you with another tool for creating melodic patterns, expand your harmonic vocabulary, define walking bass patterns, and increase your choices for expression in soloing.

The four scale groups are known as *bebop scales*. Bebop scales use a chromatic approach to create an eight-note (and eight-interval) scale. I will give some examples in the application of these scale groups, but first, let's examine the scales themselves written in the keys of F and B♭.

(mp3) 31

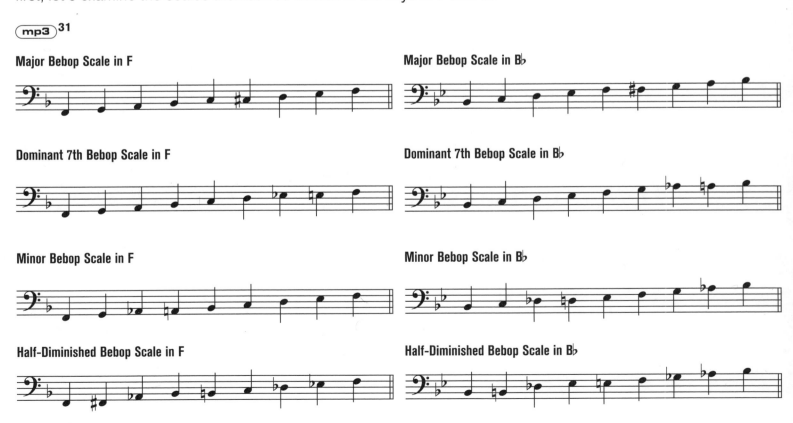

Major Bebop Scale in F

Major Bebop Scale in B♭

Dominant 7th Bebop Scale in F

Dominant 7th Bebop Scale in B♭

Minor Bebop Scale in F

Minor Bebop Scale in B♭

Half-Diminished Bebop Scale in F

Half-Diminished Bebop Scale in B♭

New Harmonic Ideas for Altered Progressions

At this point, I will concentrate on more harmonic resources for building walking bass lines and adding to your library of harmonic ideas for improvisation.

Let's look at the Rhythm Changes form again in the key of B♭. Keep in mind that the song form is A–A–B–A.

Rhythm Changes: Original Progression

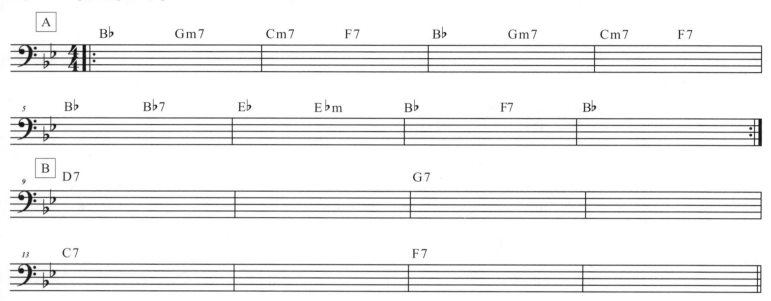

Now with that in mind, another way to view these changes is by altering the harmony, yet keeping the same form and essence of the original harmony. The interesting side of these alterations is that they really open the harmonic possibilities for walking bass lines and soloing. In the next example, we have altered the "original" form of Rhythm Changes, and this "new" progression gives us a commonly used altered form. The first two bars are very different than the original changes. Again, keep in mind that the form is A–A–B–A.

Rhythm Changes: Altered Progression mp3 32

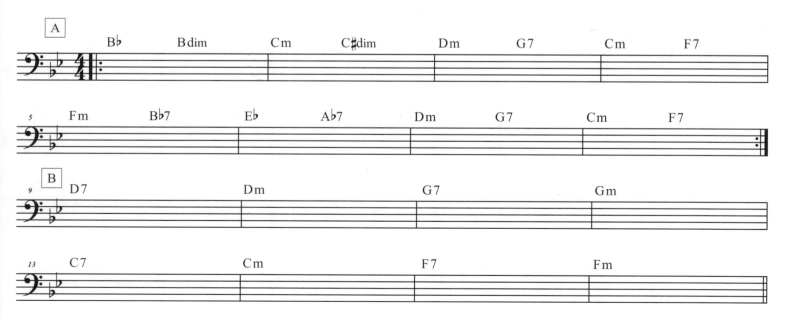

Walking Bass Lines for Altered Forms

We are now entering into the altering zone. This harmonic knowledge should, and will, increase your melodic vocabulary and definitely present you with more ideas. Also remember that any of these melodic ideas can be explored on the rhythmic level, which is always an important and interesting way to add dimension to your playing. Be aware that you can use rhythm to twist melodies around and upside-down and backwards. This will make your bass lines and solo melodies much more interesting and also help you find your own voice on your instrument.

The next example is a simple suggestion to get things started, and the B♭ major scale is a sure harmonic bet for these new changes.

B♭ Major Scale

Note that we now have a more chromatic approach with this new altered progression. The following is a sample walking bass line that is interchangeable with both the original form of Rhythm Changes and the new altered version from page 39.

In the next example, the altered form of letter A is using the altered chord progression known as the Coltrane matrix, and letter B is using a progression with tritone substitutions. This particular substitution uses a II–V turnaround just a half step up from the primary key, so you now have a II–V with the ♭9 and ♭5 in the harmony. Again, keep in mind that the form is A–A–B–A.

I've purposely superimposed the original Rhythm Changes over these altered changes so you can observe how the alternate changes create a nice dissonance when implemented. This new progression is very different from the original changes and will open you up to some very interesting walking bass options.

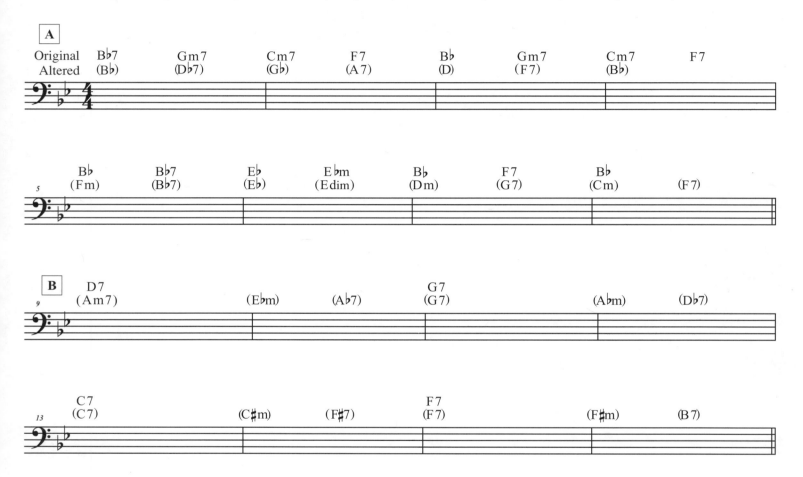

42

The next example is a walking bass line using the changes at face value. Remember to actually break the chord changes down and really examine them to discover all the melodic possibilities. This may be time consuming, but it's a great way to study harmony. I highly recommend it!

Scales for Dominant 7th Chords

I'd like to add to your melodic palette now with seven scales that deal primarily with the dominant 7th chord, which, as you can see, is extensively used in the Rhythm Changes form and blues music in general.

The following list is the dominant 7th tree of scales for the C7 chord. Please take these scales and transcribe them into every key—it's a great exercise to expand your melodic vocabulary so that you know all seven scales that correspond to each and every dominant chord possibility!

(mp3) 35

Dominant 7th Scale = C7

Bebop Scale = C7

Lydian Dominant Scale = C7(♯11) or C7(♭5)

Whole Tone Scale = C+

Diminished Scale = C7(♭9)

Diminished Whole Tone Scale = C7(♯9)

Spanish Scale (F Harmonic Scale) = C7(♭9)

These scales are great to practice and will provide many options when soloing and creating walking bass lines you can use with songs primarily or exclusively built with dominant chords—a great list of melodic tools at your disposal. You can also review the Mixolydian scales in all 12 keys, which are a typical staple for the dominant chord as a melodic color!

Diminished & Chromatic Scale Study

Here we have an interesting study of the diminished scale, which I usually view as a *double diminished* scale, meaning two diminished scales played simultaneously. This study involves the double diminished scale and the chromatic scale in relationship to one another. It will open the door for you to create and expand your knowledge of harmony and your improvisational palette, hopefully adding more to your personal music vocabulary and creatively giving you more ideas and tools for improvisation. Please feel free to refer to my book *The Melodic Bass Library,* available from Alfred Music Publishing, for more information. about a variety of scales.

The following examples were inspired by a piano book that focused on the use of the left hand, which brought in the idea of a study. Especially since a lot of piano/keyboard players I work with have a great left hand and concept for a bass line, this study brought in a different train of thought and has begun to add a new harmonic twist to my playing.

CREATING THE DOUBLE DIMINISHED SCALE

Here are a C diminished chord and a C♯ diminished chord.

C Diminished Chord

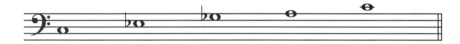

C♯ Diminished Chord

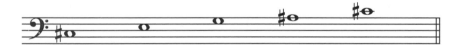

Now, if you were to play both the above diminished chords simultaneously (alternating notes of the chords), it would create a H–W–H–W–H–W–H pattern and look like this:

C Double Diminished Scale

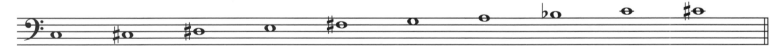

I like to work on these types of exercises, bringing in an altered sense of harmony by combining, for example, these two scales and their elements. Using altered chromatic scales in conjunction with the diminished scales will prove to do just that as well and will point you in the direction of spontaneously creating interesting melodic patterns and phrases with new ideas to add to your own vocabulary.

Study these scales and relationships methodically and you will benefit. Using a piano or keyboard to study the examples will not only help your bass playing, but also possibly open your eyes on a compositional direction as well. Improvisation is all about composition, and these elements go hand in hand.

Remember to experiment with rhythmic ideas and patterns to create variety, as well as several other dynamics that are also very important to improvisation: speed (fast and slow), volume (loud and soft), note duration (short and long), direction/movement (upwards, downwards, and multi-directional). Dynamics are three dimensional and add a lot of musicality to this study and any other study that you may be working on to improve your improvisational skills.

RANDOM HARMONIZATIONS 36

Here are some interesting two-note harmonizations using the double diminished scale. You may notice that a chromatic element has now been introduced here in parentheses. Adding these chromatic intervals will start to stretch the harmonic possibilities and open a new door for creating phrases and melodic patterns.

Double Diminished Scale with Added Chromatic Intervals

Double Diminished Scale with Chromatic Harmonization

Double Diminished Scale with Chromatic Passage in the Bass

Check out these two-note relationships. Here we simply have a diminished scale on top supported by a chromatic scale below in tandem, creating some interesting relationships and harmony.

Double Diminished Scale in Contrary Motion

This is also an interesting look at intervallic relationships, creating an interesting study. The same diminished scale, in this case a C double diminished scale, is moving in simultaneous opposition: one diminished scale moves from top to bottom, and the other moves in tandem from the bottom to the top. Again, this exercise can also be looked at on piano.

Diminished Scale with an Altered Chromatic Scale in the Bass

The next exercise, a study in single note relationships, is using the diminished scale and an altered chromatic scale simultaneously. This brings to mind what are called *alpha chords*, which are polychords that can be created here with both the Cdim and C#dim triads stacked on top of each other, arpeggiating the double diminished scale.

C Diminished Triad   C# Diminished Triad

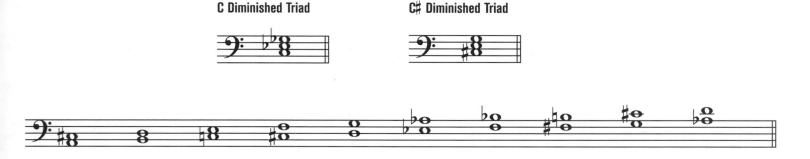

C Double Diminished Scale with a G Ten-Tone Row in the Bass

This is another exploration in intervalic relationship. All of these example have brought interesting and new ideas to play, adding more information to the improvisational pool of melodic options.

Random Intervalic Chromatic Study

Here we have a random melodic chromatic study. I find that playing this series of chromatic intervals sometimes opens me up to experimenting with harmonic patterns and structure. These exercises can also take you away from the normal practice regime, putting you in a more open frame of mind to explore new melodic options. These are some of the types of exercises that I use to open those doors.

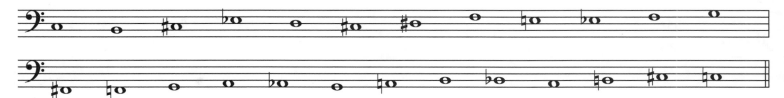

CHORD STUDIES FOR THE PIANO USING THE C CHROMATIC SCALE WITH THE DIMINISHED SCALE

C Chromatic Scale

Piano is very important for any musician to practice and study harmony! The next two exercises should be performed on piano, but they can be experimented with on bass for single-note studies. I use these exercises to practice harmony on the piano. Doing so really opens things up melodically, and on any given day, can motivate you to explore, search, and find new territory in the melodic matrix.

It is useful to work these chord studies on a piano to see the relationships between the chords and the left hand of the bass. Both use the ten-tone row shown below (with some enharmonic variations). Here, the ten-tone row is written in an obviously organized row of notes in succession, as it is based on the chromatic scale.

Ten-Tone Row

In the exercises, the notes are used in a random order to create a more interesting harmonic expression and creative progression. Make sure to study all this on piano or keyboard for interesting and useful results. I do, and normally at a very slow pace as this is a study and not a race. Please take your time with even each chord to clearly see all relationships and continually open the door for harmonic growth.

Left-Hand Piano Study with C Chromatic Scale and Chord Harmonization

Left-Hand Piano Study with Diminished Scale and Chromaticism

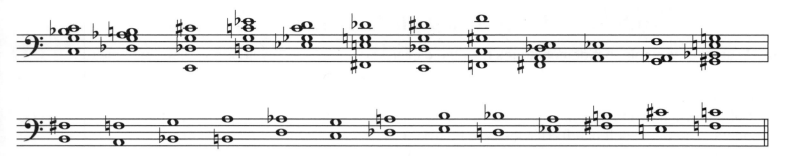

USING DIMISHED PATTERNS

The diminished scale is a very important source of melodic information. The more you practice it and get that unique sound in your ear, the more you'll find its importance in music, even in the song form of Rhythm Changes. It certainly brings an interesting color palette to the mix, and it is certain to widen your ability to express yourself in any musical situation.

I realized how heavily I rely on the diminished scale for soloing on pieces based on Rhythm Changes while performing one night with several local quartets in Los Angeles. But I found that I used it especially in the bridge section!

Here are some interesting diminished patterns in the key of E. Work on these patterns and also try to superimpose them over the Rhythm Changes bridge section. These make good exercises and will open your harmonic library to new ideas. As always, remember to expose yourself to many different kinds of music and explore as many melodic possibilities as possible in order to expand your melodic palette. Practice hard, and you will see results!

DIMINISHED PATTERNS IN THE KEY OF E MAJOR (mp3) 38

Melodic Use of the Diminished Scale: "Boomtown"

Here's another example that demonstrates how the diminished scale is a very important source of melodic info for your harmonic vocabulary. This song, "Boomtown," is from the Yellowjackets' *Mint Jam* songbook.

As you can see, the first section (eight bars long), is a vamp/A section, with a repetitive ostinato bass line, but then we move to an interesting melodic unison line that's intended to be played by the bass, saxophone, and piano (left hand). This melodic four-bar phrase is repeated, and you'll notice the diminished element in the melody of the B section, starting in the second half of the first bar.

This is a perfect example of how the diminished scale can contribute and create a unique, yet simple, melodic idea—a useful tool in composing, as you will see later in the world of improvisation.

Check out this pattern and enjoy it as an exercise for practicing.

Boomtown
Tensions

By JIMMY HASLIP &
RUSSEL FERRANTE

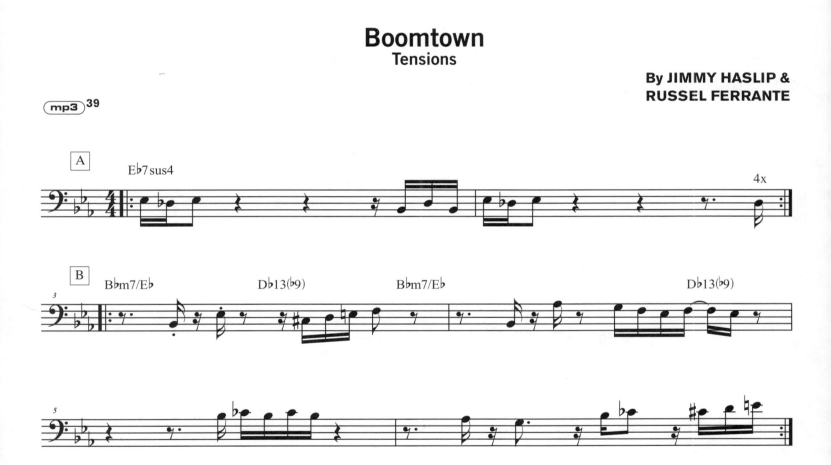

Altering the Harmony for Composition

Now let's take a bit of a side trip from my normal regulated thinking about Rhythm Changes and the II–V–I progressions.

Once, when I was composing for a Yellowjackets recording, I ventured into some experimental territory with my writing partner, Russell Ferrante. It was an exciting day of writing, as we took a very simple idea and opened the door for some interesting exploration.

I first started with a simple groove pattern in 3/4, with a drum beat and polyrhythmic bass line pattern that consisted of three notes: D, F, and C.

I also created a pulsating pedal point in octaves, in the key of D, with an interesting ethnic instrument sample triggered by a Roland 2080 synthesizer.

For the melody, Russell and I fished around for some ideas, as we had a wide-open palette to create from, and here's where it got really interesting. After searching around for an idea, I found a grouping of notes that sounded very intriguing, and I put them into a six-note scale form, hence making a scale from scratch. This gave us an unusual, yet strong, foundation for building a melody.

Synthetic Scale

It's now a finished piece of music, which features melodies played on the saxophone and piano plus an extended drum solo section.

Study this synthetic scale, and even try playing it in some different keys. Also experiment with different pedal points other than the key of D. You should realize how open this harmony is, and it may open a new door to your harmonic understanding in an altered sense!

Expanding Melodic Soloing Possibilities with the Dorian Mode

I like to study harmony through learning more songs—all kinds of songs—mostly concentrating on the melodies and looking more deeply into the chord changes as well. This is always a great way to study harmony in a very productive atmosphere, learning more about the relationships of notes and rhythms. I've found that the more songs you actually learn from top to bottom—literally—the more you will learn about harmony and the basic construction of musical pieces. It's like a form of musical anatomy!

"Milestones" is a simple song with two chord changes based on one particular scale mode: the Dorian mode. The G Dorian and A Dorian modes below will provide you with the template of harmonic information for this song.

G Dorian

A Dorian

It's always a good idea to find a great recorded version of any song you are interested in studying, and in the case of "Milestones" by Miles Davis, a great version to listen to is on the album *Milestones*, featuring Miles on trumpet, Julian "Cannonball" Adderley on tenor sax, Red Garland on piano, Paul Chambers on bass, and Philly Joe Jones on the drums. By listening to recordings like this, you will get many good, interesting ideas as well as a historical sense of the song from its origins! By focusing on a piece and thoroughly examining it from its very roots, you will build a strong foundation for improvisation.

"Stones" on the following page is a simple chart based on "Milestones." Once we look at the face value of the Dorian mode, we can look at opening the door with all the relative scales that can be used for building walking bass lines and solo improvisation. Look at this song, and find a version of "Milestones" to listen to for more study.

Stones

mp3 41

A Gm7

(4)   (8)

A Gm7

(4)   (8)

B Am

(4)   (8)

25

(4)   (8)

A Gm7

(4)   (8)

Modal Ideas for the Bridge of Rhythm Changes

Here's a typical bridge used in Rhythm Changes in B♭. As you can see, the bridge has four chords. The first chord starts on the major 3rd of the primary key of B♭ major. Note that this chord progression is referred to as the *circle of 4ths* going up in fourths, but also as the *circle of 5ths* when going down to each chord.

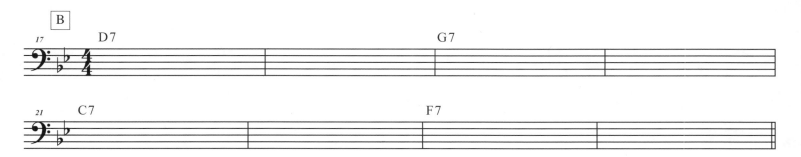

One interesting note is that, prior to each of these chords, you can add a Dorian scale, which has a minor sound, when moving to each chord, so the bridge could look and sound like this:

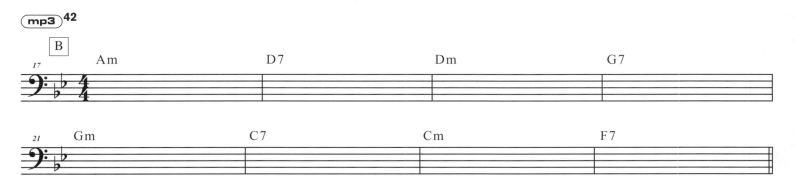

The above is a II–V turnaround. The two (II) refers to the Dorian scale, and the five (V) refers to the dominant 7th chord or Mixolydian scale. Practice playing through the chord changes with the scale cells below to find many melodic options for this interesting chord progression. You will find that many songs have these chord progressions built into the form, and it will become an extremely useful tool for playing in general!

Practice with Chordal Arpeggios

One great way to work on your soloing chops is to take groupings of three, four, five, six, or more notes and spend hours creating melodic phrases with the understanding that you must improvise the playing of these groups of notes in as many variations as you can. An infinite number of possibilities exist here, including dynamics, both the rhythm and the volume of each of the notes, different tempos, and the use of cadence, as well as the placement of notes—as in playing the note sequences forward and backwards, displacing the notes in various sequences, and even the use of different octaves.

I learned this practice regime from a few different horn players who suggested practicing this type of discipline, and also from a very important book about soloing by Marc Johnson called *Concepts for Bass Soloing*.

Here are some interesting chordal arpeggios in scale form with upper extensions, also called *tensions*, to practice and add to your own melodic library.

Work on these and any other chordal arpeggiations for more ideas. This is a very good way to open the door to being more comfortable and confident with improvisation.

"GALILEO"

Ideas on the Major Scale Inspired by Jaco Pastorius

One of the great bassists in history is the late Jaco Pastorius. I cannot say enough about this incredible and inspired musician. He was the icon for revolutionary bassists of our era, and I was honored to have been a student of his for a very short time. As short as that was, my time with him was extremely enlightening, and I would have to say that it changed my life in a big way—an unforgettable learning experience on all levels.

One aspect of music that became clearer to me was the importance of harmony. I always knew that it was important, but watching and listening to Jaco play and speak about it opened my eyes even wider. I began to really understand the major scale in more detail, and it led me into some new and interesting harmonic territories.

On the following page is a sample of what I created once I began to explore the Ionian mode (the major scale) for improvisation, soloing, and writing melodies in the key of C. "Galileo" uses the major scale within the context of the solo performed in this piece, which I wrote in honor and tribute to Jaco, from the Yellowjackets CD *Politics*.

Ionian Mode (Pattern)

Galileo

By JIMMY HASLIP

Bass Solo starting at approximately 1:50

"GABRIELA ROSE"

Here's a song from the Yellowjackets CD *Time Squared* called "Gabriela Rose." Let's look at the improvised solo from this song. It has a bit of complex harmony and took some thought to feel comfortable on the bridge progression, so let's start with looking at this entire solo. Play through this slowly and examine each phrase to determine its purpose and how it coincides with the chord changes.

mp3 46

Gabriela Rose

By JIMMY HASLIP

Melodic and Harmonic Analysis of "Gabriela Rose"

First off, there are a total of 29 bars in which I soloed—an unusual number that therefore poses a complex, yet interesting, form to create a solo that flows and has uniformity.

Let's start with the first section.

Bars 1–3: I started the solo with Cm7, which is really a setup for the actual solo section. The 1st phrase is an excerpt from the C minor pentatonic scale starting on the 5th (G), using the upper octave C to the major 3rd above (#9) down to the minor 7th, the 5th again, the 4th, the minor 3rd, and so on… This is all very straight ahead over the first chord of the solo section.

You'll notice the phrasing is juxtaposed in such a way that my last note, an F, falls on the downbeat of the next chord, F/A. So we have the root of the upper extension but not the root of the chord, which is a better choice for the harmony there. I personally like to stay away from playing any root notes on the downbeats—that's already covered by the sub bass part.

Bars 4–8: Now we go to the first bar of the solo section. This next phrase is completely constructed from an Ab major pentatonic scale, but I'm also using a Db (the 4th) to embellish the Db major sound in the harmony. As you can hear, the simple addition of the Db alters and/or extends the harmony over this Abmaj7. I continue this thought to end the phrase, again with a Db, on the downbeat of the next bar, which is a Gbmaj7 chord; the Db, now the 5th of this new chord, is the only note in the bar. This is followed in the next bar of Gbmaj7 with the same pattern of notes played a whole step down in Gb. So you then have the Gb major pentatonic scale with a Cb (the 4th).

The next phrase continues into the next bar on an Ebm7 chord, which now transforms as it shares the same notes of this upper portion of the Gb major pentatonic scale and becomes the first four notes of the Eb minor pentatonic scale. What a coincidence! You see, Gb major pentatonic and Eb minor pentatonic are relative scales as they would be diatonically related. They are really in the same system and share all of the same notes, as they are actually one and the same scale. So I would see these four bars as Gb major.

BARS 9–14

The next four staves are loaded with triplet figures, which will rhythmically add dimension and dynamics to your improvisation.

Bar 9: With Cm7 in this first bar, we have three triplet figures. I play an arpeggiated C minor scale using the root, minor 3rd, the 5th, the 7th, and the octave C, right into a C minor extension using the major 2nd (the 9th), the minor 3rd (the 10th), and the 4th (the 11th). The last note of the third triplet figure, a Db, is the root of the next chord (which has an altered bass note, a B, the 7th below).

Bar 10: Here, there is a simple but effective Db major arpeggio, which sounds nice with the altered root extending the accompanying harmony of the Db/B chord.

Bar 11: Playing over the B/A chord, I am basically arpeggiating a B major scale, which again sounds interesting with the B major chord altered by an A in the bass. I also continue these series of triplets, again adding rhythmic dimension to the phrasing.

Bar 12: At the top of this bar, I simply play a pattern derived from the combination of an ascending Eb melodic minor scale and a Persian scale, with a bluesy trilled inflection against the Eb/G chord.

Bars 13 & 14: Over the two chord changes Gbsus2 and Fm7, I play a Gb major arpeggio, again using triplet rhythmic figures with the root, major 3rd, 5th, octave, and major 7th in the first two triplet patterns over the Gbsus2. Then I continue the phrase into the next bar (the Fm7), altering the harmony somewhat by playing the #5, b9, #9, and 11th intervals.

BARS 15–20

Bars 15 & 16: With the chord Ab/E at bar 15, I use an altered scale, which could be called something other than what I am calling it; for my purposes, I call this scale a "melodic minor b2, b7 scale." I basically play this Eb altered melodic minor scale verbatim. Using the Eb as a passing tone, the notes are Eb, Fb, Gb, Ab, Bb, C, Db, Eb. Then, starting at the "and" of beat 4 of bar 15 into bar 16, I used a simple Ab melodic pattern based on a minor pentatonic scale.

Bars 17 & 18: With Ab/C, we have a melodic pattern starting on beat 3 of bar 17 using an Ab major pentatonic scale. This phrase ends with the root (Ab) and then continues into the next three bars as a complete statement.

Bars 19 & 20: Starting on beat 2 of bar 19, I play an arpeggio outlining an F Phrygian scale and then proceed to arpeggiate a Db major scale. These are relative scales, so you can view this entire passage at bars 19 and 20 as Db major.

Please continue working on your scales and melodic patterns. Try improvising with any major scale and see what melodies you can find within the scale itself. It's a good way to discover melodic phrasing.

BARS 21-29

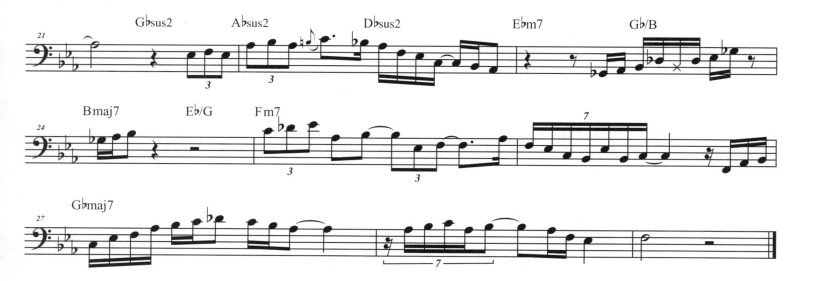

Bars 21 & 22: In bar 21, you have a G♭sus2 chord (G♭, A♭, B♭, D♭). In bar 22, you have A♭sus2 (A♭, B♭, D♭, E♭), and a D♭sus2 (D♭, E♭, G♭, A♭). As you can see, these three chords share many of the same notes, and the improvised melodic phrase is based on an A♭ major pentatonic scale (A♭, B♭, C, E♭, F, A♭). The C and F in this scale provide upper extensions to these chords. In thinking of that, you can also look at using the altered D♭ major pentatonic scale (D♭, E♭, F, A♭, B♭, C).

Bars 23 & 24: Here you have another series of chords that share a lot of the same notes. In bar 23, you have E♭m7 (E♭, G♭, B♭, D♭) and G♭/B♭ (B♭, G♭, B♭, D♭). In bar 24, you have Bmaj7 (B, E♭, B♭, A♭) and E♭/G (G, E♭, G, B♭). I chose to play phrases based on a G major pentatonic scale (G♭, A♭, B♭, D♭, E♭, G♭).

Bars 25 & 26: There are two bars of Fm7 (F, A♭, C, E♭). Here I chose to play melodic phrases based on an E♭ Mixolydian scale (E♭, F, G, A♭, B♭, C, D♭, E♭).

Bars 27–29: These contain three bars of G♭maj7 (G♭, B♭, D♭, F). You will hear phrases based on an F minor pentatonic scale (F, A♭, B♭, C, E♭, F).

Also understand that *dynamics* add dimension to your playing and, in particular, to your improvisation. This includes variations in speed, volume, rhythmic and harmonic phrasing, and directional dynamics (playing a phrase in all directions: up and down, horizontally and/or vertically).

Be sure to digest this information and practice your pentatonics often, as they are extremely useful tools for improvisation and building bass lines for all styles of music. For more info on pentatonics, check out Steve Khan's book *Pentatonic Khancepts*.

These are some of the simple tools I continually work on to improve my skill as an improviser. They are multiple-dimensional tools that offer infinite melodic and syncopated options. They also can be interpreted more articulately with variations of speed and directional dynamic alterations. It's a work and study in progress, and will be a study that ultimately changes with time and discovery. It will open doors and unlock many mysteries that may exist, and at the same time increase your vocabulary and solidify your knowledge of harmony to eliminate guess work, giving you a concrete platform to work from.

THE WHEEL OF IMPROVISATION

I use the Wheel of Improvisation to organize all my ideas. I also use it to coordinate the tools I use for improvisation and things I practice, old and new. I am constantly looking for new scales to practice, which can bring in a multitude of new ideas for improvisation.

The Wheel of Improvisation is constantly growing and being edited with new ideas while what's in there is continually re-evaluated. Learning new songs also brings in new ideas and will add new ways of improvising!

This is a visual look at what I have in my head when playing music live and in the studio.

Organizing your scales and other melodic ideas in this way will help you keep track of what you have at hand, like a virtual tool belt.

On the next page is my wheel, on which I randomly placed the scales.

BEST WISHES with YOUR STUDY and YOUR MUSIC.

Jimmy

JIMMY HASL

MODERN IMPROVISATION FOR BASS

Alfred

Alfred Music Publishing Co., Inc.
P.O. Box 10003
Van Nuys, CA 91410-0003
alfred.com

ISBN-10: 0-7390-6358-8
ISBN-13: 978-0-7390-6358-3

Front cover photo © Raj Naik • Back cover, p.2 photos © Gulnara Khamatova

Alfred Cares. Contents printed on 100% recycled paper.